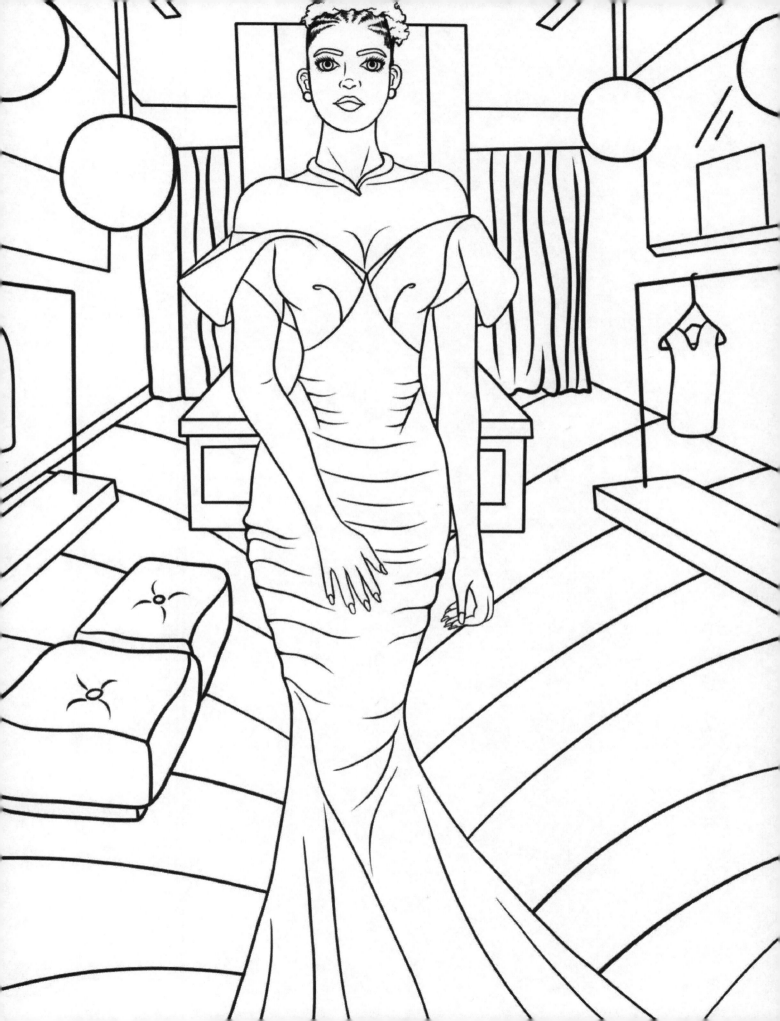

We hope you enjoyed our coloring pages inside.
We strive to provide the best possible coloring experience
and we will be deeply grateful if u would leave any kind of
feedback for our book. Thank u.

Made in the USA
Las Vegas, NV
23 June 2024

91393838R00046